Just Baking
mini pies and casseroles

Quick and Easy Single Serving Recipes
for casual family entertaining

by Robert Zollweg

Designed and written by Robert Zollweg
Photography by Rick Luettke, www.luettkestudio.com
Graphics by Gary Raschke and Robert Zollweg
Art Direction by Gary Raschke

Library of Congress Cataloging-in-Publication Data:

Just Baking, Mini Pies and Casseroles
Quick and Easy Single Serving Recipes
by Robert Zollweg

ISBN 978-0-615-61528-8

Printed in United States of America
by RR Donnelley and Company

I would like to dedicate this cookbook to

Elaine Roshong Bender

Such a great pie maker,
with caring and compassion toward others,
especially to my mother.

And to my family, for all their support,
my mother, Virginia, my kids, Christopher & Sandy, Rhonda & Doug,
their kids, Kaylie, Andrew, Bret, Morgan & Korrin

To Steven Tester, Annie, Tom Bender,
Richard & Sandy Zollweg, Judy & Carl Sims,
and all their children

My associates, Gary Raschke, who continues to put up with me
and is such a great help at putting this all together;
Sandy Shultz, Melissa Fleig, Brionna Richmond,
Fran Breitner, Amy Lewarchik, Brooks Clayton and Natalie Brunner

All my Libbey Associates:
Karen Barentzen, Beth Baroncini, Tom Fratantuono, Denise Grigg,
Cathie Logan, Gina Baccari, Jessica Adler, Kelly Kelley,
Jeff Joyce, Roger Williams, Serena Williams, Vicki Richardson,
Greg Pax, Mary Jo Conn, Mary Jane Comber, Ericka Sabo,
Brenda Bennett, Joe Mefferd and Pete Kasper

And to Libbey Glass, for giving me the opportunity to do what I enjoy doing.

Contents

Introduction

I have always loved to entertain and serving individual portions of my favorite recipes in wonderful little casseroles and baking dishes will just add something a little more special to your next dinner party. They can be used any time of the year and will add a whole new dimension to your dinner table. I felt this was something today's consumers would love and was missing in the marketplace, especially when it came to entertaining at home.

Another important feature about serving individual servings of wonderful entrees is portion control. Most of us do not need a second helping. When you have a balanced diet of wholesome foods (main entree, a starch and fresh vegetable) individual casserole servings will help maintain this balanced diet.

An even better approach to these individual servings is that you can make most of them the night before and bake what you need. With everyone's busy schedule, preparing the night before will make your dinner party just that much more enjoyable.

I hope you enjoy these wonderful recipes on individual pies and casseroles as much as I have in creating them. They are quick and simple and make a very unique presentation.

I'd like to thank all my friends, family and work associates for all their helpful ideas and input. I have learned so much about entertaining from friends and family. I love to entertain and this is a great way to turn your next special occasion into something unique and festive.

Enjoy !

Robert Zollweg

P. S. Always remember my golden rule: Entertaining is supposed to be enjoyable for you as well as your guests. So plan ahead and make it simple and make what you are comfortable with preparing. Your guests will know when you are relaxed and so will you.

Single Serving Containers

There are so many wonderful small glass or ceramic containers in the marketplace that can be used for individual pies and casseroles. Use your imagination. Use larger containers (12-16 oz) for main entree dishes, medium size ones (8-10 oz) and smaller ones (4-8 oz) for mini-tasting servings.

Many of your favorite traditional family recipes can be made in small baking dishes. Instead of putting all the ingredients in a 9x13 pan, make individual servings.

Page 12 and 13 show some of the containers I use, but feel free to experiment with others. Be creative. Almost any size baking container can be used. The recipes may need to be adjusted for large or smaller ones. All of these containers listed throughout can be purchased from various retailers. Make sure the glass and ceramic containers are all suitable for baking.

Preparation

Quick & Easy Pie Crust

Here is an easy and simple way to make a quick pie crust that is pretty good for a store purchased one. You will need one or two packages of store bought rolled pie crusts. Be sure they are at room temperature before unrolling.

Follow directions on the package. Unroll the crust on a lightly floured surface. On one side, thinly spread about a tablespoon of butter. Then sprinkle it with flour and pat down. Do the same to the other side. This will make the crust a little more flaky. Place your pie pan on the crust and trace around the dish with a knife about an 1/4" from the edge of the dish. Place the pie crust in your dish and press down. For a cream pie, prick several holes with fork all around the crust and bake for 10-12 minutes at 350 degrees. Then fill with your choice of fillings.

For a baked pie, use all the left over crust pieces to make the top crust. Piece the pieces together or make a lattice style top crust. Then fill with filling and bake as directed. Either way, it looks very homemade and delicious.

Here is another simple short cut for a pie crust. Purchase any roll of homestyle biscuits or dinner rolls. Unroll them and cut each one in half horizontally. Take the two pieces and form them in the bottom of each casserole dish. I sometimes bake them just for a few minutes, so they rise a little. Remove from oven and fill with your favorite recipe. It is great for quiches and pot pies. They wll bake better if you place them in the oven directly on the rack vs. placed on a cookie sheet. The bottom crust does not bake thoroughly on a cookie sheet.

Serving Ideas

Here are a couple of simple ideas for serving your individual casseroles at your next dinner party. Bake the main entree, starch and vegetable dishes in separate casseroles and serve them together on a larger charger or entree plate. You can also put the casserole on the dinner plate with your side dishes. Either way, your guests will love something a little different and so will you.

Fruit Pies

Apple Mince Tart

This is a little more like a cobbler than a tart because I don't use a pastry crust on the bottom. But the biscuit on top makes it quite delicious and filling.

You will need 8 small glass pie pans (4") or small ceramic casseroles. See photo at right.

Preheat oven to 350 degrees

2 cups diced apples	1 cup raisins
1/4 cup chopped pecans or walnuts	1/4 cup dried prunes and or apricots, chopped
1/2 cup orange juice	1/4 cup sugar
2 tbsp butter or margarine	1 tsp cinnamon
dash of nutmeg, cloves and ginger	1 tbsp cornstarch

one small package rolled biscuits, cut in half horizontally

1 cup vanilla yogurt or whipped topping for garnish (optional)

In a saucepan, combine raisins, nuts, prunes, apricots, sugar, cornstarch and juice. Cook over medium heat until it almost boils. Remove from heat and stir in the spices and butter. Mix well. Stir in the diced apples pieces. Mix well.

Divide the mixture equally into the individual baking dishes. Place one biscuit half in the center and press down slightly. Bake for about 20-30 minutes. Do not over bake, as the apples are better crunchy than mushy.

Cool or serve warm with a spoonful of vanilla yogurt or whipped topping. Enjoy !

Strawberry Rhubarb Crisp

When fresh strawberries are in season, nothing is more delicious. I love it plain, but most of your guests will want it with vanilla ice cream or whipped topping.

You will need 8 small glass pie dishes (4") or ceramic casseroles. See photo at right.

Preheat oven to 350 degrees

1 1/2 cups strawberries, cut into chunks
1 1/2 cups rhubarb, cut into pieces
2/3 cup sugar
1 tsp finely grated lemon peel
1/4 cup instant tapioca
2 cups flour
8 tbsp butter or margarine
1/2 cup sugar
1 tsp cinnamon

In a large mixing bowl, combine strawberries, rhubarb, 2/3 cup sugar, lemon peel and tapioca. Mix well. Divide mixture equally into the 8 pie dishes or small casseroles.

In another mixing bowl, combine the flour, 1/2 cup sugar, cinnamon and butter. Crumble together or use pastry cutter to make mixture crumbly. Sprinkle the crumbly mixture over the filling in each casserole until it is completely covered.

Place the filled pie dishes on a cookie sheet and bake for 20-30 minutes. Let cool. Serve and Enjoy !

Pumpkin Pie

What could say holidays more than fresh baked pumpkin pies? These pies are very dark in color because of all the additional spices I've added. According to my mother, the more spices the better.

You will need 8 small glass pie dishes (4"). See photo at right.

Preheat oven to 400 degrees

one large can of plain pumpkin, 27 oz   4 eggs
2 cans evaporated milk   1/2 cup sugar
1 cup dark brown sugar   2 tsp cinnamon
1/2 tsp nutmeg   1/2 tsp cloves
1/4 tsp ginger   dash of salt
1/4 cup of molasses

two packages of rolled pie crusts, see page 14
1 container of whipped topping or whipping cream for garnish, optional

Unfold the pie crusts at room temperature. Place the pie dishes on top of the crust. With a knife, cut out around dish. Place round crust in pie dish.

In a large mixing bowl, mix the eggs and sugars together. Mix in all the spices and then the pumpkin. Now stir in the evaporated milk one can at a time until smooth. Carefully fill each pie dish with pumpkin mixture until each is almost full.

Bake at 400 degrees for 10 minutes, then reduce oven temperature to 350 degrees and continue baking for an additional 40 minutes or so. When done, a table knife inserted in center should come out clean. Cool and serve with a dollop of whipped topping. Enjoy !

Apple Crumble

Fresh fruit is what makes these little pies so delicious. You will need 8 glass pie dishes or ceramic bakers, 8 oz each and preheat oven to 350 degrees.

About 12-16 apples, peeled, cored and sliced or 1 large can apple pie filling
1/2 cup flour, 1/2 cup sugar, 1 tsp cinnamon

Topping:

1/2 cup old-fashion oats	3/4 cup flour
1/4 cup white sugar	1/2 cup finely chopped almonds or pecans
1/2 cup brown sugar	1/4 tsp salt
3/4 stick butter or margarine	1 tsp ground cinnamon

In a large mixing bowl, mix together the apples, flour, sugar and cinnamon until well coated. Divide the apple mixture equally into each of the pie dishes.

For the topping: blend together the oats, flour, sugars, almonds, cinnamon, salt. Then cut in the butter using a fork or pastry cutter until crumbly. Top each of the pie dishes with the crumb mixture until covered.

Bake for 20-30 minutes at 350 degrees until bubbly and top gets slightly brown. These small pie dishes will not take very long to bake. Cool for 30 minutes and serve. Enjoy !

Cherry, Peach or Blueberry Crumble

Instead of using fresh apples, use cherry pie filing, fresh peaches or blueberries. Follow the recipe as stated above. Place the pie dishes on a cookie sheet for baking. Enjoy !

Baked Apples

Baked apples always make me feel like family. Warm and cozy. Served along with a fresh pot of tea, nothing is better after a wonderful meal. I always wait until after I've cleaned up the kitchen before serving dessert. Now I can relax and enjoy it along with my guests.

You will need 10 small glass ramekins, 6-1/2 oz each. See photo at right.

Preheat oven to 350 degrees

8-10 apples, cored and sliced (you can peel the apples if you like)
1/4 cup flour
1/2 cup sugar
1/2 tsp cinnamon
dash of nutmeg and cloves
2 tbsp butter or margarine
1/4 cup chopped pecans, delicious but optional
1 cup miniature marshmallows, optional for topping

In a large mixing bowl, combine first 6 ingredients and mix thoroughly. Divide mixture equally between the 8 small casseroles. They should be filled almost to the top. Cut the butter up into 8 slices and place a small slice on top of each casserole.

Place the casseroles on a cookie sheet. This will help in clean up in case they bubble over a little.

Bake for about 15 minutes. Do not over bake. It is better to have the apples crunchy than mushy. Remove from oven carefully. Put a heaping spoonful of marshmallows on top of each casserole. Continue baking for another 5-10 minutes or until the marshmallows are slightly melted and browned. Let cool or serve warm. Enjoy !

Classic Apple Pie

Apple pie is always someone's favorite. Serving it in a small individual pie dish just makes it more festive and delicious. Tradition in my family is going to the apple orchard, picking several varieties of apples, coming home and baking apple pies. Sandy's and Elaine's apple pies are always the first to go. So I borrowed some of their tips to make the perfect apple pie.

You will need 8 small glass pie dishes (4"). See photo at right.

Preheat oven to 350 degrees

Two packages of rolled pie crusts, see page 14 for preparation. Place round crust in pie dish and pat down. Flute the edges.

8-10 apples, peeled, cored and sliced	1/2 cup flour
1/2 cup sugar	1/2 tsp cinnamon
dash of nutmeg and cloves	2 tbsp butter or margarine

In a large mixing bowl, combine apples, sugar, flour and spices and mix thoroughly. Divide this mixture equally between the 8 small casseroles. They should be filled to a rounded mound. Cut the butter up into 8 slices and place a small slice on top of each casserole.

Take the scraps of pie crust and form another top crust using these pieces. This will be broken up and somewhat messy looking, but it will taste delicious. Place the casseroles directly on the oven rack. Put a piece of foil on the bottom of the oven to catch any drippings. This will help in clean up in case they bubble over.

Bake for about 25 - 30 minutes, until golden brown. Do not over bake. It is better to have the apples crunchy than mushy. Let cool or serve warm. Enjoy !

American Cherry Pie

The classic cherry pie just reminds me of summer days. Picking fresh cherries used to be a family thing. Today, I tend to go the easy route and buy canned cherries. This is a pretty simple version and will only take about 20 minutes to put together.

You will need 8 small glass pie dishes (4"). See photo at right.

Preheat oven to 350 degrees

Two packages of rolled pie crusts, see page 14 for preparation. Place round crust in pie dish and pat down. Flute the edges.

2 large cans of cherry pie filling
pinch of cinnamon
a few tablespoons of sugar

Fill the small pie dishes with cherry pie filling until full.

Take the scraps of pie crust and cut into strips. Criss cross them over the pie dish to form some sort of lattice top. It does not need to be perfect. Remember, this is suppose to look homemade, so if the top crust looks messy, all the better. Sprinkle with a little sugar on the lattice crust.

Place the pie dishes directly on the oven rack. Place a piece of foil on the bottom of the oven to catch any dripping during baking. This will help in clean up in case they bubble over. Bake for about 25 - 30 minutes until crust is golden brown. Do not over bake. Let cool or serve warm. Enjoy !

South Haven Peach Pie

In Michigan we have the best fresh peaches in August. Whether you make traditional pies or peach cobblers, serving them in small individual pie dishes just makes them more festive and delicious.

You will need 8 small glass pie dishes (4"). See photo at right.

Preheat oven to 350 degrees

Two packages of rolled pie crusts, see page 14 for preparation. Place round crust in pie dish and pat down. Flute the edges.

8-10 ripe peaches, peeled, cored and sliced	1/2 cup flour
1/2 cup sugar	1/4 tsp almond extract
dash of nutmeg and cinnamon	2 tbsp butter or margarine

In a large mixing bowl, combine peaches, extract, sugar, flour and spices and mix thoroughly. Divide this mixture equally between the 8 small casseroles. They should be filled to the top. Cut the butter up into 8 slices and place a small slice on top of each casserole.

Take the scraps of pie crust and form another top crust using these pieces. This will be broken up and somewhat messy looking, but will taste delicious. Place the pie dishes on the oven rack. Place a piece of foil on the bottom of the oven to catch any drippings. This will help in clean up in case they bubble over.

Bake for about 30 minutes until golden brown. Do not over bake. It is better to have to the peaches crunchy than mushy. Let cool or serve warm. Enjoy !

Mixed Berry Pie

When fresh fruit or berries are in season, this mixed berry pie takes the cake. You can use almost any combination of fresh berries. Just make sure you have enough to make about 4 cups of pie filling.

You will need 8 small glass pie dishes (4"). See photo at right.

Preheat oven to 350 degrees

Two packages of rolled pie crusts, see page 14 for preparation. Place round crust in pie dish and pat down. Flute the edges.

4 cups of mixed fresh berries (strawberries, blueberries, raspberries or blackberries)
1/2 cup flour   1/2 cup sugar
1/2 tsp cinnamon   dash of nutmeg and cloves

In a large mixing bowl, combine fresh berries, sugar, flour and spices and mix thoroughly. Divide this mixture equally between the 8 small casseroles. They should be filled almost to the top, but mounded.

Take the scraps of pie crust and form another top crust using these pieces. This will be broken up and messy looking, but will taste delicious. Or use a cookie cutter and place a piece of dough in the center as pictured. Place the pie plates directly on the oven rack. Place a piece of foil on the bottom of the oven to catch any drippings. This will help in clean up in case they bubble over.

Bake for about 30 minutes, until crust is golden brown. Do not over bake. Let cool or serve warm. Enjoy !

Strawberry Pie

During the month of June in Ohio, strawberries are at their peak and there is nothing more delicious than a fresh baked strawberry pie. Make sure you use the plump and juicy, bright red strawberries.

You will need 8 small glass dessert or pie dishes (4"). See photo at right.

Two packages of rolled pie crusts, see page 14 for preparation. Place round crust in pie dish and pat down. Flute the edges.

48 fresh strawberries, sliced   another 2 cups of chopped fresh strawberries
2 cups water   6 tbsp cornstarch
1-1/2 cups water   red food coloring

Crush 2 cups fresh chopped strawberries into 2 cups water. Cook on medium heat for about 2-3 minutes. Then mash or puree mixture until smooth. Combine the 6 tbsps of cornstarch and the 1-1/2 cups of water in a glass or shaker, mix well. Mix the two together and cook until thick and bubbly. Add a few drops of red food coloring. Stir.

In each of the individual pie dishes, fill with a heaping layer of fresh sliced strawberries. Cover with the berry puree. Place the pie plates directly on the oven rack. Place a piece of foil on the bottom of the oven to catch any drippings. This will help in clean up in case they bubble over.

Bake for 30 minutes, until crust is golden brown. When right out of the oven, garnish with a few sliced strawberries or one large one. Serve and Enjoy !

Savannah Pecan Tart

They just don't get any better than a southern pecan pie. There's something about pecans and the south that go hand in hand.

You will need 6 small ceramic casseroles or glass pie dishes, 8 oz each. I like using the low profile ones to get the thinnest tasting pecan tart. See photo at right.

Preheat oven to 375 degrees

One to two packages of rolled pie crusts, see page 14 for preparation. Place round crust in pie dish and press down. Slightly roll the edges around the edge of the dish..

3 eggs, slightly beaten
1 cup sugar
1/2 tsp salt
1/3 cup melted butter
1 cup corn syrup (dark preferred) or maple syrup
2 cup pecan halves (slightly chopped)
1 tsp dark rum or pure vanilla

1 cup whipped topping for garnish (optional)

eggs
milk
sugar
vanilla
nuts

In a mixing bowl, combine eggs, sugar, salt, butter and syrup. Stir in rum and pecans. Fill the small casseroles and bake for 30-40 minutes or until knife inserted in center comes out clean. The crust should be golden brown. Cool and garnish with a dollop of whipped topping, if desired. Refrigerate after two hours. Serve and Enjoy !

Cream Pies

Banana Cream Pie

Banana Cream Pie has been a favorite of my son, Christopher, for years, so I hope all of you will enjoy it just as much. This is a pretty quick and easy recipe using boxed pudding.

You will need 8 small glass pie dishes (4"). See photo at right.

Preheat oven to 350 degrees

One package of rolled pie crusts, see page 14 for preparation. Be sure to prick the bottom and sides with a fork. Bake at 350 degrees for 10-12 minutes. Let cool.

one large package vanilla pudding (I prefer the cooked type, because it's creamier)
2 cups cold milk
5-6 ripe bananas, thinly sliced
8 oz whipped topping or whipping cream

Layer the banana slices in the pre baked pie crusts. They should be about 3/4 full. Prepare the pudding as directed on the box. As soon as the pudding is ready, quickly fill the pie dishes, covering the bananas before the pudding sets up too much.

Let set for an hour or so in the refrigerator. When ready to serve, cover the entire surface with whipped topping or a large dollop in the center. Serve and Enjoy !

Coconut Cream Pie

Follow the recipe from above but omit the sliced bananas. When making the vanilla pudding, use 2 boxes of pudding and 4 cups of milk. Add 1 cup flaked coconut right after you put the pudding mix into the milk. Pour into each of the pie dishes and refrigerate. Cover with whipped topping. Serve and Enjoy !

Chocolate Cream Pie

Chocolate Cream Pie has been a real family favorite. Here are two versions. The first one is completely home made and the other is a pretty quick and easy recipe using boxed chocolate pudding.

You will need 8 small glass pie dishes (4"). See photo at right.

One package of rolled pie crusts, see page 14 for preparation. Be sure to prick the bottom and sides with a fork. Bake at 350 degrees for 10-12 minutes. Let cool.

Chocolate Filling

4 egg yolks, slightly beaten	1 cup sugar
1/4 cup cornstarch	3 cups milk
4 oz chocolate, unsweetened	1 tbsp butter or margarine
1 tsp vanilla	

Combine sugar and cornstarch, mix well. Gradually, stir in milk and chocolate. Cook over medium heat until thick and bubbly for two minutes. Remove from heat and stir in the beaten egg yolks. Cook another two minutes to a gentle boil. Remove from heat and stir in butter and vanilla. Mix well.

Quick & Easy recipe: use two large boxes of chocolate pudding, follow directions on box.

Pour warm chocolate mixture or pudding into each of the pie dishes with pre baked crust. Refrigerate for a couple of hours. When ready to serve, add a dollop of whipped topping or whipping cream to the center or you may cover the entire pie. Serve and Enjoy !

Berry Creams

I love to make this recipe in small dishes or glass ramekins. It's the ideal size for this wonderful dessert and makes a great presentation. You can make this recipe without the bottom graham cracker crust, but it adds a wonderful texture.

You will need 8 small glass or ceramic ramekins, 6-1/2 oz each. See photo at right.

Preheat oven to 325 degrees

2 cups graham cracker crumbs
4 tbsp butter or margarine
1/4 cup sugar

4 eggs
3/4 cup sugar
1 cup sour cream
2 cups fresh or frozen berries (strawberries, raspberries, blueberries or blackberries)

Several fresh berries for garnish, optional

Combine cracker crumbs, 1/4 cup sugar and melted butter, mix together. Spoon about two heaping tablespoons into the bottom of the glass dishes, flatten down slightly.

In a mixing bowl, beat eggs and then mix in sugar and sour cream. Chop the berries into small pieces, fold the berries into the mixture.

Divide the mixture equally into the 8 ramekins. Bake for about 30 minutes or until the custard is firm. Do not overbake. Refrigerate for an hour. When ready to serve, garnish with fresh berries on top. Serve and Enjoy !

Lemon Cream or Key Lime Pie

This recipe can be made with either lemons or limes, depending on your desire. Either one is tangy and refreshingly delicious.

You will need 8 small glass pie dishes (4") See photo at right.

Preheat oven to 325 degrees

Two packages of rolled pie crusts, see page 14 for preparation. Place round crust in pie dish and pat down. Flute the edges.

4 egg yolks
1 - 14 oz can sweetened condensed milk
1 tbsp grated lemon or key lime peel
1/2 cup water
1/2 cup fresh lemon or key lime juice (concentrate is ok, but fresh is better)
several drops of yellow or green food coloring, optional
8 very small lemon or lime wedges for garnish

8 oz whipped topping or whipping cream for garnish on top

In a glass mixing bowl, beat the egg yolks with a fork. Stir in sweetened condensed milk and lemon peel. Add water and lemon juice and a drop or two of yellow food coloring. Mix well, mixture will thicken.

Spoon lemon mixture into each of the pie dishes. Place pie dishes directly on the oven racks. Bake for 30 minutes. Cool for an hour and the refrigerate for a couple of hours before serving. Garnish with a large dollop of whipped topping and a small lemon wedge. Serve and Enjoy !

Baked Desserts

Bread Pudding

Bread pudding was never one of my favorites until I went to New Orleans a few years ago. Every restaurant I went to served it and it was as different as night and day at each place. Some serve it firm, others creamy. This one is rather firm, but some of my friends like it served with heavy cream on top. I like it with a large dollop of whipped cream. You decide.

You will need 8 small glass or ceramic casseroles, 6 oz each. See photo at right.

Preheat oven to 350 degrees

4 cups coarse french bread, cut into small bite size pieces (day old bread works best)
1 apple, cored and chopped
3 eggs, beaten
2 cups milk
3 tbsp butter or margarine, melted
1/2 cup dark brown sugar
1/2 tsp cinnamon
1 tsp vanilla
1/4 cup raisins, soaked in brandy or dark rum overnight (optional)
1 cup vanilla yogurt, whipping cream or heavy cream for garnish on top

In a large mixing bowl, mix the eggs, milk and sugar with wire whisk. Add the cubed bread, apples, brown sugar, cinnamon, vanilla and raisins if desired. Mix thoroughly.

Fill each of the small casseroles with the mixture until full. Place the casseroles in a 9 x13 pan filled with 1/2" of boiling water. Bake for about 20-30 minutes until just slightly brown. Let stand until cool or can be served warm. Serve with a spoonful of vanilla yogurt, whipped topping or heavy cream poured over the top. Serve and Enjoy !

Chocolate Bread Pudding

This recipe is something between pudding and a cake, but if you are a chocolate lover, it is right up your alley.

You will need 8 small glass ramekins or ceramic casseroles, 6-1/2 oz each. See photo at right.

Preheat oven to 350 degrees

4 cups cubed French or Italian bread
8 oz semisweet chocolate, chopped into pieces
2/3 cup sugar
4 eggs, well beaten
1 stick of butter or margarine
1 tbsp vanilla
1 cup heavy cream
1/4 cup of fudge ice cream topping and 1 cup whipped topping for garnish

In a saucepan, add cream and chocolate pieces. Simmer on low until melted and creamy smooth. You can add a little milk if needed. Add sugar, eggs, butter and vanilla and mix until smooth and creamy.

In a large mixing bowl, combine bread cubes and chocolate mixture. Gently stir until everything is well coated and mixed well.

Divide equally into each of the casseroles, filled almost to the top. Place them in a 9 x13 baking dish filled with 1/2" of boiling water. Bake for 30 minutes or until a cake tester inserted in the centers comes out with only a few crumbs. Let cool and serve with a spoonful of whipped topping or fudge topping over the top, if desired. Serve and Enjoy !

Holiday Fruitcake

A real traditional holiday favorite, especially good when served with a small glass of port wine or sherry on a cold winter's night. It is a dense dessert but bursting with flavor.

You will need 10 small glass casseroles, 6-1/2 oz each. See photo at right.

This recipe looks a little complicated, but will only take about 30 minutes to mix together. It is even better if made a few days ahead.

Preheat oven to 275 degrees

1 cup flour
1 tsp each: cinnamon, cloves, nutmeg and allspice
1/8 tsp mace and salt
1/2 cup each of raisins, dried apricots, currants, dried dates or figs, chopped pecans
1/2 cup canned pineapple tid-bits, drained
1/4 cup maraschino cherries, chopped
1 cup dark brown sugar
1 stick of butter or margarine, softened
4 eggs, slightly beaten
1/2 cup of either prune juice, grape juice, whisky or red wine
1 tsp vanilla
1 cup whipped topping for garnish (optional)

In a mixing bowl, combine flour and spices. In another large mixing bowl cream the butter and sugar together. Then add eggs, vanilla and juices. Add all fruit and nuts. The fruits should be cut into small pieces. Fold in the flour mixture and mix everything thoroughly.

Divide the mixture equally into the 8 casseroles. Place a shallow pan of water on the bottom rack of the oven. Bake the fruitcakes on the top rack for about an hour. Cool. Wrap in foil for a few days if you want or serve with a dollop of whipped topping. Enjoy !

Apple Cranberry Bake

This is one of those favorites that has been around forever. It's a very moist and crunchy cake that will really excite your tastebuds.

You will need 10 small glass ramekins, suitable for baking, 6-1/2 oz each. See photo at right.

Preheat oven to 350 degrees

1 can whole cranberry sauce
1 apple, chopped
2 cups Bisquick
1 cup sugar
1/2 cup milk
dash of cinnamon

1/2 cup brown sugar
1 tbsp flour
1 tbsp butter or margarine
1 container of whipped topping, optional

In large mixing bowl, mix the Bisquick, sugar and cinnamon together. Stir in the milk, chopped apples and the cranberry sauce. Mix well. Divide the cake mixture equally between the 8 ramekins, until about 3/4 full.

In another small mixing bowl, combine the brown sugar, flour and butter. With 2 forks, mix together to make a crumbly topping.

Cover each of the baking dishes with this crumbly topping.

Bake for 30 minutes at 350 degrees until slightly brown and a toothpick inserted in the center comes out clean. Let cool. Garnish with a large dollop of whipped topping. Serve and   Enjoy !

Spiced Fruit Pudding (Christmas Pudding)

This is one of those traditional holiday favorites that looks and tastes especially good when served in small individual casseroles for each of your guests.

You will need 12 small glass or ceramic ramekins, 6 oz each. See photo at right.

Preheat oven to 325 degrees

2 cups coarse bread cut into small bite size cubes
3 eggs, beaten
1/3 cup brandy or dark fruit juice
1/2 cup milk
1/2 cup dark brown sugar
1 tsp cinnamon and nutmeg
1/4 cup flour

1/4 cup raisins
1/4 cup currants
1/2 cup diced apples
1/4 cup grated orange rind
1/4 cup chopped pecans
1/4 tsp ginger and cloves
1/4 cup crushed pineapple

In a large mixing bowl, mix together flour, sugar and all the spices. Mix in bread cubes, fruits and nuts. Add eggs, one at a time and then mix in milk and brandy. Mixture should be very moist, add some more milk if needed.

Spoon into the ramekins until full. Bake for 20-30 minutes or until brown. Cool or serve warm with the lemon sauce if desired.

To make the lemon sauce, you will need 2 tbsp lemon juice, 2 tbsp powdered sugar, 2 tbsp butter or margarine and 1 tbsp brandy. Mix everything together, mixture should be thin and creamy, add some water if needed. Drizzle the sauce over the pudding. Pudding is best when served warm. Serve and Enjoy !

Pumpkin Cheesecake

Pumpkin Cheesecakes are one of my favorites, creamy smooth and with just enough pumpkin flavoring. These small individual cheesecake servings are ideal for buffets and after dinner desserts.

You will need 8 glass pie dishes (4"). See photo at right.

Preheat oven to 325 degrees

2 cups graham cracker crumbs, 4 tbsps melted butter, 1 tbsp. sugar

1 cup canned pure pumpkin   1/2 cup sugar
2 - 8 oz pkgs cream cheese, softened   3 eggs
1 tsp vanilla   1 tsp cinnamon
dash of cloves, ginger and nutmeg

8 oz whipped topping, optional

Mix cracker crumbs, melted butter and sugar in a mixing bowl. Divide the cracker mixture equally between the 8 dishes; press down firmly in bottom of each dish.

In a mixing bowl, mix the cream cheese, sugar and vanilla until well blended. Add the eggs and mix but do not overbeat. Remove about 1/2 the cream cheese batter and set aside. Add pumpkin and spices to other half of the mixture. Mix well.

Pour the plain cream mixture equally into the small pie dishes. Now carefully pour the pumpkin mixture on top of the cream cheese mixture. Bake for 30 minutes or until almost set. Cool and refrigerate 2-3 hours. Serve with a dollop of whipped topping. Enjoy !

Classic Cheesecake

Classic cheesecake is one of those desserts that is so delicious plain but extra tantalizing with fresh berries on top. Fresh fruit just really compliments the cheesecake perfectly.

Preheat oven to 350 degrees

You will need 8 small 6 oz ramekins or pie dishes, suitable for baking.

For a simple graham cracker crust, you will need:
2 cups graham cracker crumbs, 1/2 cup margarine, 1/4 cup sugar

2 (8 oz packages) cream cheese, softened
3/4 cup sour cream
2 eggs
3/4 cup white sugar
2 tsp vanilla
1 can of cherry, blueberry pie filling or fresh berries for topping (optional)

Mix the crust ingredients together and divide equally between the 8 dishes, press down.

Beat cream cheese, sugar and vanilla in large mixing bowl with electric mixer until well blended. Add eggs, mix again and then add the sour cream and mix thoroughly. Pour equally into the 8 ramekins or pie dishes.

Bake 30 minutes or until center is almost set. The center should jiggle just a little. Remove from oven and let cool. Refrigerate about 2-3 hours before serving. When ready to serve, top each ramekin with a spoonful of cherry pie filling or fresh berries. Serve and Enjoy !

Simple Creme Brulee

Creme Brulee is nothing more than a wonderful custard cream. Preparation is a little more time consuming, but well worth the time spent. A small individual serving is just enough of this rich and creamy dessert.

Recipe makes 6 servings in small glass or ceramic pie dishes, 8 oz each. See photo at right. Preheat oven to 325 degrees

warm together:
2 cups heavy cream
2 cups half and half
1/2 cup sugar
1 tsp. vanilla

whisk together:
6 egg yolks, slightly beaten
1/3 cup sugar
pinch of salt
cinnamon sugar or nutmeg for garnish

In a heavy saucepan, warm the heavy cream, half & half, sugar and vanilla over medium heat until hot. Do not boil. Set aside.

In a glass mixing bowl, whisk together egg yolks, 1/3 cup of sugar and salt. Combine both mixtures and divide among the 8 pie dishes. Arrange the pie dishes in a large baking dish filled with a 1/4" of hot water. Carefully transfer the baking dish to the oven. Bake custards 35-40 minutes or until just set. A knife inserted should come out clean.

Remove pie dishes from baking dish and let cool. Wrap with plastic wrap. Chill until completely cold or overnight. Remove from refrigerator 20 minutes before serving. Remove any moisture with paper towel. Sprinkle with cinnamon sugar or nutmeg before serving.

You can also add a layer of fresh raspberries or strawberries to the top instead of the cinnamon sugar or nutmeg. Serve and Enjoy!

Chocolate Raspberry Truffle Cake

This is one of those chocolate lovers dreams, a rich combination of delicious rich chocolate cake drizzled with fresh raspberry sauce. What could be more perfect?

Recipe makes 6 servings in 8 oz ceramic creme brulee dishes. See photo at right.

Preheat oven to 325 degrees

Crust:
1 cup pecans, finely chopped
1 cup graham cracker crumbs
1/4 cup butter or margarine, melted
2 tbsp sugar

Cake mix:
16 oz semisweet chocolate, cut up
1 cup whipping cream
6 eggs, beaten
1 cup sugar
1/3 cup flour

Raspberry Sauce: 1 cup fresh or frozen raspberries, 1/4 cup sugar and 1 tsp cornstarch. In a microwavable bowl, combine all the ingredients, mash together and microwave for about 2 minutes until mixture thickens. Let cool. Set aside.

For the crusts, in a glass mixing bowl, combine the first four ingredients. Divide this mixture equally between the 8 baking dishes. Press down.

In a large heavy saucepan, combine the whipping cream and chocolate pieces and cook until chocolate melts. Set aside.

In a glass mixing bowl, combine the eggs, sugar and flour and beat until lemony in color. Fold in the chocolate mixture a little at a time until completely mixed. Divide the mixture into the 8 small dishes. Bake for 30 minutes or so until the edges are puffed and the center is soft. Do not overbake. Let cool. When ready to serve, drizzle each with raspberry sauce or some fresh raspberries. Serve and Enjoy !

Breakfast Casseroles

Egg & Potato Breakfast Bake

I've been making this casserole for years, but just never called it anything. So I thought, Egg & Potato Breakfast Bake, plain and simple.

You will need 6 small oval casseroles, 8 oz each, suitable for baking.

Bake at 350 degrees for 30 minutes

4 medium size potatoes, baked, cooled and cubed
8 eggs
1/2 cup milk
1 large green pepper, chopped
1 green onion, chopped
1 cup shredded cheddar cheese
1 cup diced ham, cooked ground sausage or 1/4 cup cooked bacon, crumbled
salt and pepper to taste

Divide the cubed potatoes between the 8 casserole dishes. Add the ham, bacon or sausage, chopped green pepper and onions over the potatoes. Now sprinkle with cheddar cheese.

In a large mixing bowl, combine the eggs and milk and beat slightly. Season with salt and pepper. Divide this mixture equally into each casserole. The egg mixture should almost cover all the ingredients.

Bake at 350 degrees for about 30 minutes or until golden brown. Let stand a few minutes. Serve and Enjoy !

French Toast Souffle

There are many variations of this casserole out there today. This one is pretty simple and tasty. I like to offer different types of these souffles in small casseroles, especially for brunch, so all my family can try a few different ones.

Serve with some fresh fruit and plenty of maple syrup. I sometimes add a cup of chopped apples to the mixture before baking.

You will need 6 small casserole dishes, 10 oz each, suitable for baking. See photo at right.

one loaf of day old french bread, cubed
1-1/2 cups of dark brown sugar, divided
1 cup chopped pecans, divided
pinch of nutmeg
4 tbsps or 1/2 stick butter or margarine

2 cups of milk
1 egg
1 tsp cinnamon

In a large mixing bowl, combine the milk, egg, 1/2 cup dark brown sugar. Mix well. Stir in spices and 1/2 cup pecans. Add the bread cubes and mix until well coated and slightly soggy. Fill each of the small casseroles with the French Toast mixture.

Melt the butter in the microwave in a measuring cup. Add the cup of dark brown sugar and stir until it forms a thick sauce.

Sprinkle each casserole with the remaining pecan pieces and drizzle each with some of the brown sugar sauce. Bake in the oven for about 25-30 minutes until golden brown. Serve and Enjoy !

Egg Souffle

I borrowed this recipe from my sister-in-law, Sandy. I've changed it slightly to work with these individual casseroles, but it's basically the same. With her large family, she makes it all the time.

Bake at 350 degrees for 30 minutes.

You will need 6 to 8 small casseroles, 6 oz each. See photo at right.

one tube of refrigerated biscuits or rolls
one loaf of day old French or Italian bread, cut up or cubed, about 4 cups
1 cup cooked sausage or crumbled cooked bacon
6 eggs
1 cup milk
1-1/2 cups shredded cheddar cheese
1 cup of chopped mushrooms, green pepper or tomatoes (optional)
salt and pepper to taste

Unroll the biscuits. Cut each biscuit in half horizontally. Place both pieces in the bottom of the small casserole and press down to cover most of the bottom.

Fill each of the casserole dishes with bread cubes and some sausage.

In a large mixing bowl, combine the eggs and milk. Whisk together. Fold in one cup shredded cheese and any other ingredients you like. Salt and pepper. Pour this mixture over the bread cubes and sausage until covered.

Bake for 30 minutes until golden brown. Right after removing from oven, sprinkle with remaining shredded cheese. Serve and Enjoy !

Texas Egg Casserole

This recipe is similar to a Texas style omelet, but served in a dish. This is another one of those casseroles that is great for brunch or family get togethers. The French Toast Souffle is a great compliment to this recipe, served with a bowl of fresh fruit.

You will need 6 small casseroles, 8 oz each that are suitable for baking.

Bake at 350 degrees for 30 minutes

6 eggs
1 cup cooked sausage, crumbled cooked bacon or cubed ham
1 cup milk
1-1/2 cups shredded cheddar cheese
2 cups of chopped mushrooms, green pepper, tomatoes and green onions
salt and pepper to taste

(If you like a little zip, add a hot pepper, chopped)

Divide the fresh vegetables and sausage or bacon equally between the 6 casseroles. Sprinkle with 3/4 cup shredded cheese.

In a large mixing bowl, combine the eggs and milk and beat slightly. Season with salt and pepper. Divide this mixture equally into each casserole. Sprinkle with remaining shredded cheese.

Bake at 350 degrees for about 30 minutes or until golden brown. Let stand a few minutes. Serve and Enjoy !

Spinach Quiche

Individual quiches are so wonderful for brunch. You can make this recipe with almost any flavor or vegetable you want. I've adapted it in the past with mushrooms, bacon or ham, asparagus or broccoli. A combination of everything is pretty good also.

You will need 6 small glass pie plates or ceramic bakers, 8 oz each, suitable for baking.

Bake at 325 degrees for 30 minutes

Make pie crusts from biscuits on page 15, place biscuit in bottom of pie dishes, shape or form to sides of dish. Bake for 10 minutes until puffy, remove from oven and let cool.

8 eggs
2 cups fresh spinach
1 cup sour cream
2/3 cup cooked bacon, about 8 slices chopped
2/3 cup shredded mozzarella cheese
1/2 cup shredded swiss cheese
1/2 cup milk
1/2 cup chopped onion
dash of nutmeg
salt & pepper to taste

In a large mixing bowl, mix the eggs and sour cream together. Mix in the milk. Add the remaining ingredients and mix well. Pour mixture into the pie dishes until almost full. Tap down slightly to remove any bubbles. Bake at 325 degrees for about 30 minutes or until knife inserted in center comes out clean. Let stand a few minutes before serving. Enjoy !

Dinner Casseroles

Five Cheese Macaroni & Sausage

Here's an American classic with an added twist. Nothing is more comforting than a dish of macaroni and cheese. An individual casserole makes just the right amount for dinner or for a single serving. Make it ahead of time or freeze some servings for later when you are in a hurry. These are even great to take for lunch.

You will need 4 large casseroles, 13 oz each, suitable for baking. See photo at right.

Bake at 350 degrees for 45 minutes, or until golden brown.

12 oz pasta, either elbow, butterfly or shell
1/2 lb cooked sausage, sliced or chunked (optional)
1/2 cup chopped green pepper
1/2 cup chopped and drained tomatoes (optional)
3 cups shredded cheese (cheddar, swiss, parmesan, provolone, monterey jack)
1-1/2 cups milk or evaporated milk
1 tsp chopped fresh or dried basil
salt and pepper to taste

In a large mixing bowl, combine the milk and cheeses (save a 1/2 cup of cheese for topping). Add the pasta, green pepper, sausage, basil and salt and pepper. Mix well. For easy cleanup, spray your casseroles with a non stick cooking spray before filling. Divide mixture equally between the casserole dishes. Sprinkle with remaining shredded cheeses. Bake in oven at 350 degrees for about 30 minutes until top is golden brown and bubbly. Serve and Enjoy !

Chicken Pot Pie

I love these pies, fresh out of the oven and piping hot. They really hit the spot. This is a pretty versatile casserole. I've always made them with chicken, but you can use beef and vegetarian style.

You will need 8 small pie dishes (4") suitable for baking.

Bake at 350 degrees for 45 minutes, or until golden brown.

2 large cooked chicken breasts, diced
1 can evaporated milk
1/2 cup sliced carrots
1/2 cup frozen corn
1 tsp basil
salt and pepper to taste

2 pkg. refrigerator rolls, see page 15
1/2 cup fresh green beans, chopped
1/2 cup frozen peas
1/4 cup flour
1 tsp tarragon

Follow page 15 for the biscuit dough bottom crust. Do not pre-bake. Make sure the dough comes up the sides of the pie dish.

In a large mixing bowl, combine the condensed milk and flour. Whisk until smooth. Mix in the vegetables and chicken. Add the spices and mix well. Fill the pie dishes with the mixture. Take a small piece of biscuit dough and form a small flattened ball and place it in the center of the casserole as pictured. Sprinkle with some fresh ground pepper. Bake at 350 degrees for about 30 minutes or until golden brown. Do not place on cookie sheet, the crusts do not bake thoroughly. Instead place a piece of foil on the bottom rack to catch any drippings for easier cleanup. Let cool just a few minutes before serving. Enjoy !

Chicken & Broccoli Casserole

This is almost a complete dinner in one. Creamy and delicious and pretty healthy. It is one of my favorites and we have been making it for years in my family.

You will need 4 large casseroles, 13 oz each, suitable for baking. See photo at right.

Bake at 350 degrees for 45 minutes, or until golden brown.

2-3 chicken breasts, cooked or grilled and cubed
one large bunch of fresh broccoli, cut into small bite size pieces
2 cups shredded swiss cheese, divided
1/2 cup cracker crumbs
1 can cream of mushroom soup
1/2 cup milk
salt and pepper to taste

Divide the cubed chicken and chunked broccoli equally between the 6 casseroles. Sprinkle with the shredded Swiss cheese. Salt and pepper.

In a mixing bowl or large measuring cup, mix together the mushroom soup and milk until creamy smooth. Pour mixture over the chicken and broccoli. Sprinkle each casserole with additional shredded cheese and then with some cracker crumbs. Bake in oven at 350 degrees for about 30 minutes. Do not over bake, you want the broccoli firm not mushy. Serve immediately. Enjoy !

Scalloped Potatoes and Ham

My kids and family grew up on this casserole. It is a little more time consuming, because I use fresh, sliced potatoes instead of the frozen ones. It works great as a leftover or made the day before.

You will need 6 small round casseroles, 10 oz each, suitable for baking. See photo at right.

Bake at 350 degrees for 45 minutes, or until golden brown.

8 - 10 medium size potatoes, thinly sliced
2 cups of chopped ham
2 cans of cream of mushroom soup
2 cups milk
several stalks of celery, finely chopped
one onion, chopped
salt and pepper to taste
one cup of cracker crumbs, optional

Wash the potatoes, leaving the skin on. Thinly slice and place in cold water until ready to mix together. In a large glass mixing bowl, mix together the mushroom soup and milk until creamy. Stir in the celery, onions and ham. Salt and pepper to taste.

Drain potatoes and divide them equally between the 8 casseroles. Pour the soup mixture over the potatoes until covered. Sprinkle with cracker crumbs, optional.

Bake for 45 minutes until brown and bubbly. Serve and Enjoy !

Tuna & Noddle Casserole

This is as old as your grandmother and just as wonderful and delicious. There are a million variations and I'm sure they are all fantastic. This recipe has been in my family for years.

You will need 6 small casseroles, 15 oz each, suitable for baking. See photo at right.

Bake at 350 degrees for 30 minutes, or until golden brown.

1 lb noodles, cooked as directed on package
1 large can of tuna fish packed in water, drained well
1 can cream of mushroom soup
1 cup milk
1 small onion, chopped
1 cup finely chopped celery
salt and pepper to taste
1 cup cracker crumbs for topping, optional

Sometimes I add a package of frozen peas

In a large mixing bowl, combine the mushroom soup and milk, whisk together. Add the tuna, onion and chopped celery, mix together. Add the cooked noodles and mix together.

Fill each of the casseroles with the noodle mixture until full. Sprinkle with some cracker crumbs on top and bake in the oven at 350 degrees for about 30 minutes and golden brown. Serve hot. Enjoy !

Shepherd's Pie

Shepherd's Pie is an old English favorite from years ago. The whole idea here was to use leftovers from your English pot roast that will be made into another delicious dinner. There are many variations of this famous dish. Here is one of them.

You will need 6 small round casseroles, 10 oz each, suitable for baking. See photo at right.

Bake at 350 degrees for 30 minutes, or until golden brown.

3 cups cooked potatoes, you can use mashed, boiled, sliced, fried or hash browns
2 cups cooked roast beef, ground beef or chicken pieces
1 cup frozen corn, thawed or green beans or both
1/2 cup sliced carrots, fresh or frozen
1/2 cup chopped onions or green onions
1/2 chopped celery
3 tbsp butter or margarine
1 cup shredded cheddar cheese, optional
salt and pepper to taste

In a large skillet, saute the vegetables (onions, corn, green beans, carrots and celery) in the butter for a few minutes until tender. You can also microwave them for a few minutes.

In each casserole, add a layer of shredded meat and the sauted vegetables. Salt and pepper to taste. Cover each of the casseroles with your choice of potatoes about a half inch thick or so. Sprinkle with the shredded cheese.

Bake in oven at 350 degrees for about 30 minutes or heated through. Serve and Enjoy !

Pasta Fasoli

This is one of my favorite casseroles. I use it a lot when I'm having the card club over. It's a complete meal. All you need is a nice fresh garden salad, some french bread and dinner is ready. You can make them ahead, even the night before. This is a little spicy, but most everyone today likes their food a little spicier. Put aluminum foil over each casserole and keep them refrigerated until ready for the oven.

You will need 4 large oval casseroles, 13 oz each. See photo at right.

Bake at 350 degrees

12 oz pasta, cooked
1 lb Italian sausage, cooked
1 large can of diced or stewed tomatoes, 22 oz.
1 can kidney beans
2 lb shredded cheddar cheese, divided
1 cup parmesan cheese, divided
one small onion, chopped
1 green pepper, chopped

In a large mixing bowl combine all ingredients except 1/2 cup of shredded cheese and 1/2 cup parmesan cheese. Divide the mixture between the casserole dishes. Sprinkle with the remaining shredded cheeses. Bake in the oven for 30 minutes, until hot and bubbly. Remove and let stand a few minutes before serving. Enjoy !

Quick & Easy Italian Lasagna

You will find this recipe a little different because I don't use lasagna noddles. I use any small style shell or butterfly pasta or extra wide plain noodles. But you can use the standard lasagna noodles if you want. It is just easier to work with smaller pasta in the small individual casseroles and also much easier to eat.

You will need 4 large oval casseroles, 13 oz each. Bake at 350 degrees.

1 lb extra wide noodles or pasta	1 lb ground cooked beef or sausage
1 onion, chopped	1 lb ricotta cheese or cottage cheese
8 oz mozzarella cheese	1 egg, slightly beaten
1/2 cup fresh parmesan cheese	1 large can tomato sauce
1 large can of stewed tomatoes	1/2 cup finely chopped green pepper
2 garlic cloves	1 tsp thyme
1 tbsp oregano	1 tbsp tarragon
1 tbsp basil	salt & pepper to taste

For vegetarian lasagna, substitute 3-4 fresh sliced zucchini for ground beef

Prepare the noodles as directed on package but only cook about 7 minutes. They need to be al dente (firm). In a skillet or pot, add the cooked ground beef, onion, both tomatoes, green pepper and all spices. Simmer for about an hour or so. In a large mixing bowl, combine the egg, ricotta and parmesan cheeses. Mix well and set aside. A jar of prepared sauce (Ragu) will work when you are short of time.

Put a large spoonful of sauce in the bottom of each casserole. Add a layer of noodles or pasta, a layer of sauce, then the cheese mixture and some more pasta. Cover with another spoonful of sauce. Cover the top with shredded mozzarella cheese.

Bake at 350 degrees for 30 minutes, let stand about 5 minutes before serving. Enjoy !

Enchilada Supreme

This traditional Mexican-American casserole can be made either hot or mild, depending on how spicy you like things. I always make mine kind of mild and serve it with some hot sauce or salsa on the side. I let my guests adjust it to their taste.

You will need 4 large oval casseroles, 13 oz each, suitable for baking. Bake at 325 degrees

6 corn or flour tortillas
1 lb cooked ground beef, turkey or shredded chicken
2 cups shredded colby or cheddar cheese
1 jar or 2 cups enchilada sauce or regular salsa
1 small onion, finely chopped
1 green pepper, finely chopped
1 cup chopped lettuce
1 can refried beans, optional
non stick cooking spray
some sour cream and hot sauce on the side, optional

Lightly spray each of your casseroles with cooking spray. Put a spoonful of enchilada sauce on the bottom. Place a tortilla shell flat on the table, spread about a tablespoon of refried beans, fill it with your choice of meat, lettuce, onion, green peppers and a heaping spoon of enchilada sauce. Roll up and place in the casserole. Repeat this until you have 2-3 enchiladas in each casserole. Cover with enchilada sauce and shredded cheddar cheese.

Bake in oven at 350 degrees for 30-35 minutes until bubbly. This casserole is ideal when served with fresh salad and Mexican rice. Serve with sour cream and hot sauce on the side. Enjoy !

Deep Dish Pizza

This is one of my favorites. Once you put the crust in the casserole dish, you can add almost any thing you want to create your own personal deep dish pizza. These are great for parties and you can let your guests create their own.

You will need 6 large ceramic casseroles, 8 oz each. See photo at right.

1 large package of refrigerator dinner rolls, see page 15

1 cup pizza sauce or brush with olive oil

a variety of vegetables, chopped into pieces; green peppers, onions, banana peppers, mushrooms, black or green olives,

some meats; cooked ground beef or sausage, pepperoni, ham or chicken

1 cup shredded mozzarella cheese

Cut a biscuit in half, horizonally and press into the bottom of each casserole. Add a heaping tablespoon of pizza sauce to the bottom and spread around. Now layer any of the vegetables and meat you like, finish with a layer of mozzarella cheese

Place all the casseroles directly on the oven rack and bake for about 20 minutes at 350 degrees until brown and bubbly. I do not recommend using a cookie sheet, it keeps the crust from baking completely. Serve and Enjoy !

Soups & Sides

French Onion Soup

Bubbly French Onion Soup, with lots of cheese on top, is what life is all about. My granddaughters are really hooked on this soup. You might be also.

You will need 6 crocks or round casseroles 10 oz., suitable for baking. See photo at right.

4 large onions, thinly sliced
2 tbsp butter or margarine
2 tsp flour
4 cups beef broth
salt and pepper to taste
1 cup grated or shredded mozzarella cheese
1/4 cup grated parmesan cheese
2 cups of toasted bread cubes or boxed croutons

In a large deep skillet or pot, melt the butter. Add the onions and saute until they are lightly colored. Stir in the flour and cook until the onions are a darker brown color. Be careful, not to burn. Add the beef broth and stir. Cover the pan and let simmer for about 30 minutes.

Ladle the hot onion soup into each of the crocks to about 3/4 full. Fill with toasted croutons. Pour a little more broth over the croutons. Sprinkle generously with shredded mozzarella and a little parmesan cheese. Place the crocks on a cookie sheet and place in the oven set at 350 degrees for 15 minutes. Then turn the oven to broil and broil for 5 minutes or so until the cheese is golden brown and bubbly. Serve immediately. Enjoy !

Baked Veggie Corn Chowder

This is an ideal soup course before serving your main entree. You can make it ahead of time and have it in the oven while everything else is getting ready. Serve it with a handful of oyster crackers and you are ready to go. Serve it for lunch with a small side sandwich. Either way you will love it.

You will need 6 round crocks or casseroles, 15 oz each and suitable for baking. Bake in oven at 325 degrees. See photo at right.

2 cans of evaporated milk
2 cup cooked potatoes, cubed
1/4 cup of finely chopped onion
1/4 cup flour
1/2 cup shredded Swiss cheese
salt and pepper to taste
1 cup of cooked diced chicken, optional

2 cups frozen corn, thawed
1 small carrot, finely chopped
1/4 cup of finely chopped celery
1/4 cup of finely chopped green or red pepper
1/2 cup of bread or cracker crumbs

You can also use 2 cups of mixed vegetables instead of 2 cups corn.

In a large mixing bowl or pan, whisk together the milk and flour. Add the corn, potatoes, onion, carrot, celery and green pepper, mix well. Salt and pepper to taste. Pour into each of the crocks until almost full. Cover the top with cheese and bread crumbs.

Bake in oven at 350 degrees for 30 minutes until hot and bubbly. Serve and Enjoy !

Mixed Vegetable Bake

This is one of those side dishes that is quick and easy but very delicious. Making it in individual casserole dishes just adds to the festivity.

You will need 6 small oval casseroles, 8 oz each, suitable for baking. See photo at right.

Bake at 350 degrees for 30-35 minutes, or until golden brown.

1 cup fresh green beans	1 cup carrots, sliced
1 cup frozen corn	1 cup frozen peas
1 cup baby lima beans	1/2 cup chopped water chestnuts
1/2 cup chopped celery	1/2 cup chopped green pepper
1 small onion, chopped	1 cup chicken broth
1/2 cup flour	1 cup shredded swiss cheese
salt and pepper to taste	

1 cup cracker or bread crumbs or canned fried onion rings for topping, optional

In a jar or sealed container, mix the cold chicken broth and flour. Shake until thick and creamy (a can of cream of mushroom soup will also work).

In a large mixing bowl, combine all the vegetables, water chestnuts and shredded cheese. Mix in the chicken broth mixture. Divide the mixture equally between the 6 casseroles. Salt and pepper to taste. Sprinkle each of the casseroles with some bread crumbs. They do not need to be covered completely.

Bake the casseroles on a cookie sheet at 350 degrees for about 30-35 minutes or until golden brown and the vegetables are tender. Enjoy !

Au Gratin Potatoes

Au Gratin potatoes made with real fresh sliced potatoes is so delicious, but I've used frozen hash brown potatoes when I'm in a hurry. Nobody will really know the difference if you don't tell them.

You will need 6 small oval casseroles, 8 oz each, suitable for baking. See photo at right.

Bake at 350 degrees for 30 minutes, or until golden brown.

About 10-12 potatoes, scrubbed, sliced and unpeeled
1 cup milk
1/2 cup flour
1/4 cup cooked bacon, crisp and crumbled
1 cup shredded cheese, cheddar, Swiss or provolone
salt and pepper to taste

In a large mixing bowl, combine all the ingredients and mix well until completely covered in sauce mixture. Divide mixture equally between the casserole dishes.

Bake in oven at 350 degrees for 30-40 minutes until potatoes are tender. Use a fork to test for tenderness. Serve immediately and Enjoy !

Sweet Potato Souffle

Sweet Potato Casserole is one of my favorites recipes during the holidays, but is really delicious almost anytime of year. It's pretty simple to make and adds a different twist to traditional potato side dishes.

You will need 6 small casseroles, 10 oz each, suitable for baking. See photo at right.

Bake at 350 degrees for 45 minutes.

two 28 oz cans of sweet potatoes, drained or 6 sweet potatoes peeled and cooked
2 cups dark brown sugar, divided
1/4 cup milk, cream or half and half
1 stick of butter or margarine
1 cup pecans, finely chopped
1/4 cup of honey or maple syrup

In a large glass mixing bowl, mash up the sweet potatoes and the milk. Stir in one cup of brown sugar. Mix thoroughly. Divide the potato mixture equally into each of the small casseroles.

In another microwavable bowl, melt the butter. Stir in the honey and pecan pieces. Place a heaping spoon of pecan mixture on top of each of the sweet potatoes.

Bake for 30-45 minutes until hot. Serve and Enjoy !

Texas Baked Beans

This is my adaptation of baked beans that I have been making for years. I like to add a variety of different beans for a unique texture and flavor. But you can just use navy beans or pork and beans if you want the traditional style baked beans. Serving baked beans in little casseroles is a unique way to serve side dishes. It is a little different, but it is just so much fun and adds a different twist to your dinner or buffet presentation.

You will need 6 casseroles, 15 oz each, suitable for baking. See photo at right.

Bake at 350 degrees for 45 minutes.

one 28 oz large can of baked beans or pork and beans, drained
one 15 oz can of kidney beans, drained
one 15 oz can of northern beans, drained
one 15 oz can of black beans, drained
one green pepper, chopped
one large onion, chopped
3 tbsp mustard
3 tbsp ketchup
2 cups dark brown sugar

In a large mixing bowl, mix all the ingredients together. Be sure the beans are well drained, otherwise the beans will be soupy. Divide the beans equally into each of the small casseroles. If you have some left over, put in a storage container and save for later. Bake for about 45 minutes until thickened and slightly browned on top. Let stand a few minutes and serve. Enjoy !

Columbus Baked Beans

My niece, Kiki Zollweg in Columbus, Ohio, gave me this recipe. It is extraordinary. It has been in her family for years and now our family is in love with it. This bean dish could almost be served as a main dish, it is so hearty and rich with flavor. This recipe makes quite a lot of baked beans, more than enough to fill these 8 small casseroles for single servings with lots of extra.

You will need 6 small casseroles, 10 oz each, suitable for baking. See photo at right.

1/2 lb sausage, browned
1/2 cup celery, diced
1 small can spicy chili beans
1 can black beans
1 can green beans
1 can kidney beans
1 can tomato sauce
1 cup dark brown sugar

1/2 lb ground beef, browned
1 onion, chopped
1 can Bush's baked beans
1 can lima beans
1 can wax beans
1 can tomato soup
1 tbsp mustard

Be sure to drain all your beans except the chile and Bushs Baked Beans, otherwise the mixture will be too soupy.

In a large pan, saute both meats, onion and celery until brown. Add chili and Bush's beans, the drained remaining beans. Add the tomato soup and sauce, mustard and brown sugar. Mix thoroughly. Fill each of the casseroles until full.

You will have extra. Store in the refrigerator in a sealed container.

Bake at 350 degrees for 35-45 minutes until hot and bubbly. Let stand few minutes before serving. Enjoy !

Scalloped Corn

My family has always loved scalloped corn during the holidays. But you can also substitute other vegetables in place of corn. Try using green beans, peas, asparagus or cauliflower or any combination of them. They will add a real twist to your next get together.

You will need 10 small casseroles, 6 oz each, suitable for baking. See photo at right.

Bake at 350 degrees for 45 minutes

1 egg
1 cup evaporated milk or sour cream
1 cup bread crumbs, corn bread or cracker crumbs, divided
3 cups frozen corn, thawed
1/4 cup green and red pepper, finely chopped
2 tbsp pimento (optional)
4 tbsp melted butter or margarine
salt and pepper to taste

In a large glass mixing bowl, beat the milk, egg, salt and pepper. Mix in 2/3 cup bread or cracker crumbs. Stir in the corn, green peppers, pimento and chopped onions.

Divide the mixture equally between the small casseroles. Drizzle a little melted butter over each casserole. Sprinkle with bread or cracker crumbs.

Bake uncovered for 30 minutes, let stand a few minutes and serve. Enjoy !

INDEX

About the author.

ROBERT ZOLLWEG has written numerous cookbooks and books on home decorating and has been in the tabletop industry for almost 40 years. He designs glassware, flatware and ceramic products for the retail and foodservice industry. He has worked with all of the major retailers from Bed Bath & Beyond, Crate and Barrel, Williams-Sonoma, Macy's, Pier One Imports, Cost Plus World Market, JCPenneys, Target, Walmart, Home Outfitters and Sears, to name a few. He has worked most of his professional career for Libbey Glass in

Toledo, Ohio. He has traveled the world extensively looking for color and design trends and the right product to design and bring to the retail and foodservice marketplace. He is also an artist-painter and works primarily with acrylic on canvas using bold primary colors. He currently lives in his historic home in Toledo's Historic Old West End and in the artistic community of Saugatuck, Michigan.

To know more about Robert Zollweg,
visit his web site at
www.zollwegart.com

Just mini Cocktails

cocktails & party drinks

Fun & Exciting Cocktail Recipes
for casual entertaining
and tasting parties
by Robert Zollweg

Creative accents
home décor ideas with glass

Decorative Home

Wedding & Bridal

Holiday Centerpieces

Young & Modern

Craft Ideas

Fun & Exciting Home Décor
decorating ideas with
glass centerpieces
by Robert Zollweg

HOME décor
creative ideas with glass

Decorative Accessories
Wedding & Bridal
Holiday Centerpieces
Young & Modern
Craft Ideas
Bed & Bath

Fun & Exciting Home Décor
decorating ideas with
glass centerpieces
by Robert Zollweg

Just Tasting

mini appetizers
soups & salads

Quick and Easy Recipes
mini appetizers soups & salads
by Robert Zollweg   for casual entertaining

CRAFT BREWS
the right glass for the right beer

ales and lagers
beer cocktails
by Robert Zollweg   food pairing with craft beers

Just Baking
mini pies and casseroles

Quick and Easy
Single Serving Recipes
by Robert Zollweg   for casual family entertaining

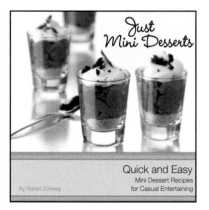

Just Mini Desserts

Quick and Easy
Mini Dessert Recipes
by Robert Zollweg   for Casual Entertaining

I hope you have enjoyed my cookbook on Just Baking. It's all about individual portions, for yourself or for your guests at your next dinner party.

Any of my cookbooks or home décor books would be a wonderful compliment to anyone's home entertaining cookbook collection. They are all available at area retailers or on my web site at:

www.zollwegart.com

Enjoy !   Robert